Building Self-Confidence

Nancy Tune

A LifeSchool™ Work Text

Fearon Education
Belmont, California

Simon & Schuster Supplementary Education Group

ISBN-0-8224-4368-6
Printed in the United States of America
1. 9 8 7 6 5

Contents

Introduction

Modern life can be very hard. There aren't enough jobs. Prices keep going up. Most people live in a rush, trying to keep up with school or a job or both. Often people live far from their families. Sometimes neighbors do not know each other.

In all of this it can be very hard to have a clear idea of who you are and how you fit in with the world around you. Almost everyone has had the feeling of being lost in the crowd.

Often people dream of a better life. They wish for the time and money to do the things they enjoy. They wish that they could feel close to the people they see every day. They want to feel good about their lives.

There are probably people around you who seem to have what you want. These people seem to do well and are happy most of the time. If you asked these people for the secret to their happiness, you would get different answers: "I love my job." "My family makes me happy." "I take care of my health." "I work hard for what I want." These are all things that make people happy. But one thing that is the same for all these people is the way they see life. The people who get along best believe that it is possible to solve their problems. They believe in themselves.

There is a big difference between people who believe in themselves and people who believe that they can't make it. But people are not born with this difference. They learn to see (or not to see) the good things in life. They learn to feel good about themselves.

In this book you will read about the things you need in order to feel good about yourself. In each chapter you will find some examples of problems that people face. You will learn how these problems hold people back, and you will read about steps you can take to solve the problems. As you work through the steps at the end of each chapter, remember that they are not ways of getting rid of problems. They are ways of working with problems. Remember, too, that there is more than one right way to follow each step. Every step you take that helps you is a right step.

Chapter 1
All About Confidence

Gina is lucky. Everyone says so. She is smart and pretty. She has lots of friends. She gets along well with her family. She has been living at home for a year while she saves money for junior college. Next month she will start classes. Most of her friends have not been able to save enough money for school. Everyone thinks that Gina has it made. Everyone but Gina.

Gina knows what people think about her. But she also knows how she feels. Gina did well in high school. But she picked many classes that were easy for her. She isn't sure that she can do the work in college. She has heard that the social life will be different in college, too. Her old friends won't be there with her. Will the college kids like her? Gina's father might lose his job. He wants Gina to get a part-time job to help out. Gina is afraid that a job will make things even harder for her.

Gina would love to talk to someone about this. But she doesn't know who. She has always laughed and joked with her friends. That's why they like her. If she tells them how bad she feels now, they probably won't understand her problems. Gina thinks they might not like her anymore. So no one but Gina knows how she feels.

Gina has a problem. She's scared. She is afraid that she won't fit in with a new group of people. She is afraid that she will not be able to do what other people expect of her—and what she expects of herself. Gina's **self-confidence** is very shaky right now.

Words to Learn

self-confidence (or **confidence**) a feeling of having trust in yourself; a feeling of being sure of yourself

self-confident (or **confident**) having trust in yourself; being sure of yourself

The Meaning of Self-Confidence

You probably have a good idea of what self-confidence is. You might call it feeling sure of yourself or feeling proud of yourself. You might call it liking yourself the way you are. You know that when you feel **self-confident** you feel good. You get along well with the people around you. You can get your work done. You can take care of problems and still feel all right.

You probably also have a good idea of how you feel when you are not self-confident. You might feel shy, lonely, worried, and maybe even angry. Everything seems harder when you are not sure of yourself.

There are two important things to remember about these feelings. One is that everyone has them. The other is that you can change them and help yourself to feel better.

Everyone Has Problems

It is often hard to believe that other people have trouble with self-confidence. When you see someone like Gina, you feel sure that she is confident. And yet people like Gina often find it hard to talk about their problems. What this shows is that you know how *you* feel, but you don't know how everyone else feels.

Self-confidence is something that you have been learning since you were a baby. You are still learning it now. You can learn a math fact or how to spell a hard word, and after you do you can count on those things. They don't change. But you do change. And so does everyone and everything around you. No wonder it's hard to feel sure of yourself all the time. This is true for everyone. You can be sure that everyone has trouble with self-confidence at least some of the time.

It is not hard to understand what self-confidence is and why everyone has trouble with it. But sometimes it is hard to know what you can do to build your self-confidence.

Words to Learn

success something you do that turns out very well

successful how you feel when you have success

Success and Confidence

Think about the times when you have felt sure of yourself. Chances are they were times when you had a **success.** Confidence comes from being **successful.** Each time you have a success, you feel good about yourself. The more successes you have, the better you feel about yourself. Have you ever scored a touchdown? Have you ever gotten a perfect score on a test? These things make people feel good about themselves. But no one can have big successes all the time. Very few people ever score a touchdown. Even the best players don't score a touchdown in every game. And even the best players may not feel successful *off* the playing field.

Think of the times when your self-confidence has been very low. These probably were times when you felt that you had failed or were going to fail. In real life, everyone fails some of the time. How can you keep the feelings of success even when you are having trouble or are afraid? That is one of the hardest things people have to do.

The Confidence Circle

In a way, self-confidence is a circle of feelings and actions. When you are successful, you feel confident. When you feel confident, you are more likely to be successful again. When you do not feel confident, you get into another kind of circle. If you believe that you will fail, you are more likely to fail. When you do badly, you feel bad about yourself. Getting into a circle of success and staying there is something that most people try hard to do for much of their lives.

Words to Learn

self-image the idea or picture you have of yourself in your mind

ability the know-how to do something well

What Everyone Needs

Being confident is a healthy state of mind. Your body needs certain things to stay healthy: good food, rest, exercise, and so on. Your mind needs certain things to stay healthy, too.

These are the most important things you need in order to feel confident.

- A good **self-image.** Your self-image is the way you "look at" yourself. In order to have a good self-image, you need to see yourself as a good person.
- The **ability** to do things. Most people need to believe that they can do some things well. It feels good to have abilities and to know how to use them.

Words to Learn

goals things that you aim for and try to get

- **Goals** to work for. Goals are plans that you work to carry out. Suppose you plan to finish a job by the end of the day or to change jobs by the end of the year. These are goals. When you make a plan and carry it out you prove to yourself that you can make things work out as you want them to.
- Good connections with people. The way other people see you tells you a lot about yourself. That is why it is important to get along with other people in your life. Everyone needs the feeling of belonging that comes from being comfortable with other people.
- The ability to live with changes. Changes are hard on most people. But everyone must deal with many changes in his or her life. The better you are at facing changes, the more comfortable you will feel about your life.

Some people seem to have an easy time with the things listed above. These people seem to be lucky, just as Gina does. Good luck can help. But everyone can have the things that are needed for self-confidence.

It takes a lot of work. But the work is worth doing. A feeling of self-confidence will help you with every part of your life—doing your job, getting along with people, and even having fun.

You have to take only one step at a time. As long as you are working on the things that hold you back, your self-confidence will grow. As long as your self-confidence is growing, you will feel and act better. You will be building your own circle of confidence and success.

Exercises

1. Look at the Words to Remember on this page. Then fill in each blank below with the right word to complete the sentence.
   a. Success and feeling good about yourself leads to a circle of ______ .
   b. When you know how to do something well you show that you have ______ .
   c. The way you see yourself is your ______ .

2. Darken the circle next to the *best* answer. Self-confidence starts with ______ .
   ○ being lucky
   ○ hard work
   ○ lots of money
   ○ joking and laughing

3. Write two or more sentences to explain why each of these things help you to have self-confidence:
   a. Good friends. ______________________
   b. Jobs you can do well. ______________________
   c. Plans for the future. ______________________

4. Write two or more sentences to explain what this saying tells about self-confidence: *Nothing succeeds like success.*
   ____

Words to Remember

ability
goals
self-confidence (or **confidence**)
self-confident (or **confident**)
self-image
success
successful

Chapter 2

It's All in Your Mind

November 16

Dear John,

Forget our skiing trip. I have terrible news. I lost my job. My boss, Mr. Potter, said it was because I just started work — last hired, first fired. He was pretty nice about it. But I must have done something wrong. Nothing like this has ever happened to me before. It's a total disaster. Mr. Potter said he can help me find another job. But there's no way. No one hires people who just got fired. Go ahead and make plans to ski with someone else. Right now I don't have enough money for the bus ride. Sorry about this.

Alex

Adams Industries
2140 Baker Road
Baltimore, Maryland

November 16, 1985

To Whom It May Concern:

This is to recommend Alex Garcia for work as a forklift operator. Mr. Garcia joined Adams Industries just two months ago. He has done fine work for us from the start. Because of budget problems here at Adams, we have had to let go the five workers we hired in September. It is our bad luck that Mr. Garcia is one of those people. In the short time he was here, Mr. Garcia was one of our hardest workers. He learned his job quickly. He took directions well. He stayed with each task until it was finished. I recommend him strongly.

James B. Potter
Warehouse Supervisor

On November 15, Alex Garcia was told by his boss that he had lost his job. On November 16, Alex wrote a letter to his friend John. The same day, Alex's former boss wrote a letter to help Alex get a new job. The two letters tell different stories about what happened.

Feelings and Facts

The letter Alex wrote shows how he feels about losing his job. He is sad and upset. Anyone would be. It is bad luck to lose a job. Alex feels more than unlucky. He feels as if he has failed. But Mr. Potter's letter gives a different idea about Alex. It makes Alex seem special.

Take a minute to read Alex's letter again. Which things does Alex know for a fact? He knows that he has lost his job. He knows that has never happened to him before. He has very little money. These things are true.

Which things in Alex's letter tell what Alex thinks but are not facts? He says that he must have done something wrong.

Words to Learn

attitude the way you feel or think about someone or some thing

positive helpful and hopeful, the opposite of negative

negative not helpful or hopeful, the opposite of positive

Mr. Potter can't help him. No one hires people who have been fired.

If you look at just the facts, Alex does have a big problem. But is it a "total disaster"?

Alex's biggest problem is that he doesn't believe in himself. His **attitude** could hurt him even more than losing his job. Attitude is the way people look at themselves and the people and things around them. Two people with different attitudes can see the same thing in different ways.

Positive and Negative Attitudes

You may have heard something like this: John and Mary can look at the same glass of water. John says it's half full, but Mary says it's half empty. John and Mary have different attitudes. John thinks about what is there. Mary thinks about what is missing. The person who sees the cup half full usually has a **positive** attitude. The person who sees it half empty usually has a **negative** attitude.

Your self-image is your attitude toward yourself. It can be positive or negative. Alex has a negative self-image right now. He thinks that losing his job was his fault. He thinks that he can't do anything to help himself. Another worker who lost his job might say, "This is rotten luck. Now I'll have to start to look for another job." This way of thinking doesn't pretend that losing your job is good news. But it leaves room for making things better.

Like Alex, many people feel that each problem tells them a lot about themselves. They see their problems as facts that can't be changed. This kind of negative thinking can get to be a habit. When people fall into the habit of looking at the world in a negative way they block their chances for success.

Finding the Circle of Confidence

In Chapter 1 you read that being confident works in a circle. In the same way, failure can become a circle of negative feelings and actions.

Alex was in a negative circle when he wrote to his friend. He felt that he had failed when he lost his job. His self-image became very low. When he looks for a new job, his lack of self-confidence may show. He won't be able to tell other people why they should hire him because he doesn't really believe that they should. As long as Alex has a negative attitude, he probably won't get a good job.

No one wants to fail. But everyone fails some of the time. How can you keep from getting into a habit of failure?

Suppose Alex read Mr. Potter's letter. He might see himself differently. He might remember the good things that he did at work. He might believe that other companies would want him. Then he would have a better chance of finding a new job. Even if Alex never saw that letter, there are things he could do. He could make a list of the good things he did when he worked for Mr. Potter. He could think of the best way to tell other bosses those things. He could call Mr. Potter and ask about other companies where he might look for work. By taking such actions, Alex would show a positive attitude. He would give himself a chance to succeed.

Everyday Problems with Self-Image

Suppose you don't have a problem like Alex's. Most of the time, you get along fine. But you don't always feel confident. You might have a problem with your self-image. Read the three examples below. Think about the ways in which these people are like Alex—and like you or someone you know.

1. Jan was taking a course in night school. She did not do well on her first test. She was embarrassed. She started to miss classes. After a few weeks, she dropped out of the course.
2. Mark wishes that he looked better. He feels he is too short and wishes he wasn't beginning to lose his hair. Last week he asked a woman he works with to have lunch with him. She said that she had other plans. But Mark is sure that she would have gone with him if he looked better.
3. Carol went to say hello to Jane, her new neighbor. Someone else arrived just as Carol did. It was an old friend of Jane's. Carol stayed only a short time. As she left, she heard Jane and her old friend laughing. Carol was sure that they were laughing at her.

Jan, Mark, and Carol all have negative attitudes toward themselves. They all believe that they are not as good as the people around them. Their attitudes have become habits they don't even know they have.

Breaking Habits

Suppose you want to break a bad habit such as talking too much or biting your nails. You know that you have to stop doing a certain thing. If you try hard, you can learn to catch yourself each time you start to do that thing. You find something else to do instead. For example, if you want to quit biting your nails, you might chew gum instead. But if your problem begins in your mind, how do you stop it?

You can break any habit in the same way. The first step is in your mind. You must *want* to change. You must believe that you can change. After that, you take action. You catch yourself when you are doing or thinking things that are bad for you. You try to stop. You try to do or think about things that will help you instead. You practice changing habits by doing the helpful things over and over again.

When you are trying to change the way you see yourself, the hardest part might be knowing when you are doing the wrong things. Think of the examples of Jan, Mark, and Carol. What action can these people take to change their attitudes?

Jan thinks that one bad grade means she has failed in class. She needs to tell herself that this is not true. She should go back to class and find out what she did wrong on the test. She could talk to her teacher. She could get help from a classmate. She could read more or practice more. If she tries hard, things will become clearer for her.

Mark needs to stop thinking about his height and his hair. Other people may not even see those things when they look at him. He needs to think about his good points and not worry about what others might be thinking.

Carol should know that there are a lot of reasons that two old friends could have for laughing together. It is not at all likely that they were laughing at her. She should go back to see Jane soon, and not stay away because she feels bad about her first visit.

Here are some steps you can take to help make your own attitude more positive. As you read these steps, keep your thinking habits in mind. Which steps should you start to use? Which ones could you take more often? Practice these steps and turn them into habits.

Be fair to yourself. When you do something well, do you think of ways that you could have done it better? When you do something badly, do you remember it for months? You are not being fair to yourself. The next time you remember an embarrassing moment or a failure, stop yourself. Think about something good you have done. It doesn't have to be something that many people know about. It could be a big, messy job that you finished. It could be a time when you helped a friend with a problem. It could be a hard class in school that you got through. Make a list of these things. Look at the list from time to time and add to it when you can. Keep the good things in your mind to balance the bad ones.

Use good sense. Do you sometimes feel that people are talking about you? If you make a mistake, do you think that others remember it and hold it against you? The next time you have such thoughts, stop yourself. Think of all the things that people could be talking about besides you. Think of all the times you have seen other people make mistakes. Do you think of the mistakes every time you see the people? It is not likely that the people around you are spending a lot of their time thinking about your mistakes either. Everyone is much too interested in his or her own life to do such a thing.

Words to Learn

solution the way in which a problem can be solved

Use the right words. "I did *everything* wrong! I'll *never* get over it! It was the *worst* thing that could have happened!" Was it really? Everyone has to deal with terrible things in life at some time. But most of the problems that people have are not terrible. They can be bad. They may spoil an afternoon or a day or even a week. But they do not ruin a job or a friendship or a life. Try to use words that describe things the way they are. "I was embarrassed about the mistake I made today. Now I'll have to do some extra work to fix things up." Words like these help you remember that you can take action to solve your problems.

Think of solving your problems. When you have a problem on your mind, sometimes it's hard to think of anything else. The next time this happens, try to face the problem in a different way. Think about how to start to make it better. Here is a plan for solving most problems:

1. Figure out just what the problem is.
2. Think of some possible ways the problem could be solved.
3. Decide what would happen if you tried each **solution.**
4. Choose the best solution.
5. Take action.

If the problem is big, break it into smaller parts. Then work on one part at a time.

See yourself in the best possible way. Most people are not completely happy about the way they look. When you look in a mirror, do you see one or two things that you don't like? If they are things you can change, start to work on them. Dress more neatly. Stand up straighter. Smile more often. If they are things you can't change, try to stop worrying. Remember that other people don't think about things such as how much hair you have or how tall you are every time they look at you. They think more about what you are like to them—a neighbor, co-worker, or a friend.

If you practice these steps until they become habits, you will change your self-image. Most change is not a steady climb. Sometimes it goes very well. Other times it doesn't work out the way you wanted it to. But as long as you are working on positive change, your self-image will keep getting better.

Exercises

1. Look at the Words to Remember on this page. Then fill in each blank below with the right word that completes the sentence.

   a. Your ______________ is how you feel about something.

   b. If you work to make things better, you are acting in a ______________ way.

   c. When you want to solve a problem, you look for a ______________ .

2. Darken the circle next to the *best* answer below.
   Which of the following can you change by your attitude?

   ○ your height
   ○ your self-image
   ○ your family background
   ○ how you do your job

3. Darken the circle next to each right answer below.
   Which of the following must you do in order to change a habit? You must ______ .

   ○ want to change
   ○ be told to change
   ○ take action
   ○ have no problems

4. Darken the circle next to the sentence in each pair that shows a *positive* attitude.

   ○ I'll probably get fired for that mistake I made at work today.
   ○ I know now why I made that mistake at work today.

   ○ I never did like school; but I know I need a high school diploma in order to get a good job.
   ○ I wish I could get a high school diploma; but I'm just not the type for school.

5. Write two or more sentences to explain what this saying tells you about attitude: *You are your own worst enemy.*

   ____
   ____
   ____
   ____
   ____
   ____
   ____

Words to Remember

attitude	negative	positive	solution

Chapter 3

You Can Do It

Maggie believed that she was a good person. Most of the time she had a positive self-image. But when she applied for her first full-time job, she ran into trouble. She couldn't think of a single skill she had. Maggie's friend Karen also was looking for a job. She made a list of three skills that she felt she could use. When the two talked about what they had written, Maggie was surprised. She had grown up with Karen. The two had done many of the same things. How could Karen come up with a list of skills when Maggie couldn't think of any?

Name: Maggie Kato
Address: 16 Parkside Dr.
Phone: 444-1711

Interests:
Traveling to other countries; reading about foreign countries.

Skills:

I verify that all the information on this application is true.

Signed: Maggie Kato

Name: Karen Maxwell
Address: 17720 Rancho St.
Phone: 234-5789

Interests:
Playing the piano; Studying Art.

Skills:
Working with elderly people; operating cash register; keeping organized files.

I verify that all the information on this application is true.

Signed: Karen Maxwell

Words to Learn

skills things that people can do well

Different Kinds of Skills

Maggie was thinking of **skills** in the wrong way. She was thinking only of certain job skills, such as typing or welding. These are useful and important skills. But they aren't the only or most important skills that a person can have.

In order to be confident, you have to think of yourself as a person who can do things. Most people think of certain jobs when they think of what they can do. When you are a child, people ask what you want to do when you grow up. When you are in school, people ask what you will do when you graduate. When you have finished school, you often hear the question, "What do you do?" These questions are all about jobs.

It's not surprising that people pay so much attention to jobs. Most people spend one-third of their waking hours at a job. People depend on their jobs to pay for food, housing, and clothes. People often make good friends at work. They can get a lot of satisfaction from a job they enjoy. Many people's self-images are formed by the way they see themselves in the working world. So having job skills is an important part of self-confidence.

But the skills you use off the job may be just as important as the ones you use on the job. For example, Karen's skills were not learned at work. She often visited her grandmother in a nursing home. She talked and read to the other patients while she was there. She also learned to operate a cash register for a school fair. And she helped her parents keep the files of family papers. Some people wouldn't think of these things as job skills. But Karen knew they were useful abilities.

By talking to Karen, Maggie learned that she, too, had some useful skills that she had never thought about before. Maggie was the oldest child in her family. Her parents worked long hours. So Maggie had to help run the house. These are some of the things she knew how to do well:

1. She kept a list each week of all the food the family needed.

2. She shopped for the food. She found the best price for everything she bought.

3. She taught her younger brothers to do many of the chores around the house. She made up games so they would have a good time while they worked.

4. Maggie often fixed broken things around the house. She also made simple toys for her brothers.

Words to Learn

compliments nice things people say about other people

After Maggie made the list, she started to feel better about herself. She also found out some things about herself. She realized that she did not like keeping house and shopping. She did enjoy taking care of her brothers and their friends who came to play. She remembered that many people had given her **compliments** on how well she took care of the children. People thought a lot of the games and songs that Maggie made up and taught to the young children. Thinking of this made Maggie feel even better. It made her see that her skills were real and useful.

Finding Your Skills

Many people have not had all the experiences Maggie and Karen have. If you have not, you might have to work harder to make a list of skills that you have learned. If you think that you can't even make a list, you might need to work on your attitude. In Chapter 2 you read that a negative attitude can make you feel you are not as good as the people around you. If you really believe that you have no skills, your attitude is a problem. Perhaps, like Maggie, you are not thinking of skills in the right way. Almost certainly, you are not thinking of yourself in the right way. Read the steps on pages 15–16 of Chapter 2 again.

You may have heard the joke about the patient who asks a doctor, "Will I be able to play the piano after the operation?"

The doctor says, "Of course."

And the patient says, "That's great! I was never able to play it before!" In real life people have to develop skills on their own. It's hard work, starting with developing a positive self-image. But the good news is that everyone can do it.

Practice the following suggestions. They will help you start to believe in and build your abilities.

Think about your good times. Think of the times when you are happiest with yourself. Make a list of the things you do at those times. Don't be afraid to write "playing ball with friends" or "listening to music alone." Then think of projects you have worked on when you felt good. Have you planned a party? Made a repair by following directions? Taken part in a sports event? Learned to play a musical instrument? Taught someone else to do something? Write down anything that might fit this list.

Double-check your list. Ask yourself this about each entry on your list: Does this help me feel good about myself? Playing ball with friends probably does make you feel good about yourself. You are part of a team. You are valued for your skill at the game, for your ability to work with a team, and maybe for your sense of humor. But if you have listed "sleeping until noon," that item probably does not help your self-image. Cross it out and think of something better to take its place.

Make a list of jobs. Choose one item on your list. Write down everything that you do connected with that item. For example, suppose the item is helping to plan a surprise party for a good friend. In order to do that you probably would have had to do some or all of these things: plan the date, time, and place; plan the guest list; invite the guests; choose the refreshments; decide who will bring each kind of food (or make the food yourself); buy decorations; keep the guest of honor away until the right time; and help everyone have a good time at the party.

Name your skills. For each job you wrote down, think of the skill or skills you used to get the job done: planning ahead, dividing up tasks, buying on a budget, cooking, using your imagination, and making people feel at home are just a few skills that go with the examples above. They are skills you can use in every part of your life. Now choose another item on your list. See whether the same skills come up again or whether you have a long list of separate skills. Either way is fine. This is useful information to have about yourself.

Take your skills with you every day. Don't separate your skills in one area from the rest of your life. Learn to think of the things you can do as you go through each day. Don't be afraid to show what you can do. Maybe you can give good directions to help people find their way. Maybe you can speak more than one language. Maybe you can teach children how to draw or swim or play soccer. The more you use all your skills, the more confident you will be of them.

Give yourself full credit. Do you ever answer a compliment by saying, "Oh, that wasn't hard. Anyone could do that." If that were true, you probably wouldn't have gotten the compliment. Take credit. Say thank you when you get a compliment. Keep the good feeling in mind.

Learn to give yourself compliments too. If you have signed up for a night class for the first time, you have made an important step. Don't tell yourself that other people could do it easily. If it was hard for you, and you did it anyway, give yourself a pat on the back.

Do something new. Have you ever said things such as, "I don't think I'll go because I'm not very good at baseball" or "I can't do that because I'm no good at fixing things"? Trying new projects or jobs can be very difficult. You have to be willing to make mistakes while you are learning. You have to be willing to practice and practice. No one likes to struggle for new skills. But it is bad for you not to try. Being afraid to try new things can become a negative habit. Work little by little to build new skills.

Do something now. Action is an important key to making your life better. If you're not a welder, you can't go out and start welding tomorrow. But you can start to work on your skills right away. Plan your day tomorrow so that it will be more active than today. Instead of watching TV, for example, write a letter. Or get a room ready for painting. Or go to a movie with a friend. Plan to do one new active thing every day for a week. After that you might want to add more things. Or you might find something that you want to do often. Being more active will help you feel better about your abilities and yourself.

Exercises

1. Look at the Words to Remember on this page. Then fill in each blank below with the right word that completes the sentence.

   a. ______________ are the things that people can do well.

   b. When people do a good job at something, they should receive ______________ for their work.

2. Darken the circle next to each right answer. In order to be confident, you need ______ .

   ○ a positive self-image
   ○ to be better than others
   ○ a job that pays a lot
   ○ to know that you have skills

3. Suppose you had to fix a leaky pipe under a sink. Darken the circle next to all the skills below that you might need to do the job correctly.

   ○ plan a job ahead of time
   ○ understand written directions
   ○ know which tools to use
   ○ solve problems that you don't expect
   ○ know how to balance a checkbook

4. People should keep developing new skills, even if they are happy with themselves. Do you agree or disagree with this statement? Write two or more sentences explaining the reasons for your answer.

   ____
   ____
   ____
   ____
   ____
   ____

5. Pick two jobs or tasks that you feel you do well. Then list three skills that you have that enable you to do each job or task correctly.

   ____
   ____
   ____
   ____
   ____
   ____

Words to Remember

compliments **skills**

Chapter 4

Know Where You're Going

Carla: I'm thinking of quitting my job. I'd like to work at home. That way I could decide what hours to work. I really like the idea of being my own boss.

Dan: I think of quitting my job every day. I want to spend the next six months on a warm beach!

Lisa: As long as we're dreaming, I think I'll go to Hollywood. Maybe I could get a job in the movies.

Carla: I'm not dreaming. I mean it. I want to work for myself.

Dan: I wouldn't want to work for myself. But it might be great for you. You should talk to someone who owns his own business. Find out what it's really like.

Carla: I've already talked to a few people. But I still need more information. I think I'll be ready to make the change in about six months.

Lisa: It's great to plan ahead like that. Sometimes I have trouble planning one day at a time.

Dan: I'm great at planning ahead. I make plans all the time. I'm just not very good at carrying them out.

Lisa: I'm not bad at carrying out small plans. But I have trouble with the big ones.

Dan: Like being in the movies?

Carla: Well, for now, Hollywood can wait. I think we'd better plan to get back to work.

Carla was making real plans for herself. She had already started to work on her plans. But the things that Lisa and Dan were talking about were dreams, not real plans. It's fine to dream about what might happen. But of these three friends, only Carla will probably reach her goal. When you want to make a change in your life, dreams have to be turned into action.

Words to Learn

future the time that is ahead

motivation the cause or reason for a person to act in a certain way

Goals and Motivation

Think about the real-life plans you make for yourself. Some are for the next day or two. Some are plans for the **future**—for two months or two years from now. Some plans are for small things, such as cleaning out a desk or writing an important letter. Other plans are much bigger, such as training for a certain job or having a family. All of these plans are goals. They are things that you plan and then work for. When you set your goals and then meet them, you show that you plan well and get things done. You feel successful and good about yourself.

Have you ever heard someone say, "I have no **motivation**"? Motivation is the push you need to get things done. It is the feeling of wanting to do something. Without motivation, it's hard to do anything. Goals help to motivate you. When you decide on a goal, you can see where you are headed. That helps you to see what path to take to get there. And when you know the way, it's easier to take the first steps.

Words to Learn

realistic having to do with things that are real and practical

short-term covering a short period of time

long-term covering a long period of time

Setting Good Goals

Your goals also are important because they can help you see what your interests are or what you believe in. For example, if you love music, you might set a goal to learn to play an instrument well. If family life is important to you, one of your goals might be to be a good parent. You are motivated to reach these goals because they mean a lot to you.

The best goals for you are the ones that you set for yourself. Sometimes people have goals that are not completely their own.

For example, your teachers and your family all want you to be successful in school. This is a good goal, but be sure that it is important to you, too. If you try to reach a goal that you don't believe in, your motivation will be low. You will have a hard time moving toward the goal. And that will be hard on your self-confidence.

It is important to set your own goals. It also is important to set goals you can reach. In the conversation at the beginning of this chapter, Dan and Lisa were joking about their plans for the future. But many people do set goals that are not **realistic.** If a goal is not realistic, it may be impossible to reach. For example, the goal of acting in movies is a dream for many people. It is realistic for only a few. If a goal is not realistic, it can be bad for you. You might keep the goal in mind but never work toward it. You might try to reach the goal but never come close. Either way, your confidence will suffer.

Short-Term and Long-Term Goals

Everyone needs to set two kinds of goals. There are goals that keep you moving through your day-to-day life. These might include finishing a task at work or painting a room at home. These are called **short-term** goals. You can finish them fairly quickly.

Other goals are set far in the future. These are goals such as learning a new skill, finding a better job, or buying a house. They are **long-term** goals. Often these goals are like dreams. They seem far off. It is hard to know what to do each day to work toward them. But if they are realistic, you will be able to make a plan and work toward your long-term goals.

Both kinds of goals are important to your self-confidence. Meeting your short-term goals is one way of using your skills. It helps you prove to yourself and to the world that you have abilities. And it helps give you the confidence to work on your long-term goals. Long-term goals give you a greater sense of self-worth. You are not a person who lives only from day to day. You have beliefs and ideas about who you are and how you will grow in the future.

The key to holding the good feelings that your goals can give you is to take action. Begin to work toward your goals. You can start by taking the steps listed below.

Make a list of your goals. Don't be afraid to write down goals that seem very small. And for now, don't throw out big goals because you aren't sure you can reach them. Take your time and give this list careful thought. Then divide the list into short-term and long-term goals.

Break down the short-term goals. Look at your short-term goals. How many steps will you have to take to finish each one? Some will take only one step. Others will take several steps. For example, if you want to paint a room, you might have to buy supplies and prepare the walls before you begin to paint.

Use a separate piece of paper to list the steps for each goal. Next to each step, write down how long you think it will take to do it.

Break down your long-term goals. Almost everyone makes the mistake of setting some goals that are too far away. Most long-term goals need to be broken down into smaller goals that you know you can reach. Suppose you have a goal of being a manager where you work. What steps can you take now to work toward that goal? One step might be to get a good review from your boss. What steps will lead to that? Think about the things you do each day at work. You might make a plan to do some of those things faster or better. List each long-term goal on a separate piece of paper. Keep working until you have a list of steps you can take for each goal—day by day or week by week.

Check your goals again. Ask yourself these questions:

- Is it *your* goal? Is it important to *you*?
- Is it realistic? Can you reach it?
- Is it a good goal? Will you be better off when you reach this goal? Will you feel good about yourself as you work toward it?

If you answer *no* to these questions, you will probably want to think about changing the goal.

Start working on your goals. When you have finished your list, don't put it away. Start to work. Put the short-term goals in order, starting with the one that you will finish first. Begin to work on it today. Then look at the steps for the long-term goals. Take at least one of those steps in the next week. When you take a step, cross it off or put a check next to it. Add any new steps that you think of as you go along.

Expect to change the list. Suppose you don't reach one of the goals you set. Or you take a number of steps toward a goal and then decide that it is not a good goal for you. It doesn't mean that all of your goals are wrong. It may just mean that you are not ready for that goal right now. Maybe you need more time for some steps. You should expect to change your list as you go along. The important thing is to keep moving toward goals that you believe in.

Exercises

1. Look at the Words to Remember on this page. Then fill in each blank below with the right word that completes the sentence.

   a. If a goal is not ________________, it might not be possible to reach it.

   b. When you believe in a goal, you will have the ________________ to work for it.

   c. ________________ goals should be broken down into smaller jobs that you can work on from day to day.

2. Darken the circle next to each right answer. The best goals are ones that ______ .

   ○ you believe in
   ○ you probably won't reach
   ○ are realistic
   ○ are only dreams

3. Joe has a dream of being a pilot. He is not sure if this is a good goal for him. Darken the circle next to the *first* thing Joe should do.

   ○ Sign up for flight school.
   ○ List the steps leading to the goal.
   ○ Choose another goal that will be easier.
   ○ Take a ride in an airplane.

4. Mary has always wanted to be a nurse. After one year of nursing school, she does not like any of her courses. Darken the circle next to the *first* thing Mary should do.

   ○ Drop out of school.
   ○ Force herself to finish school.
   ○ Figure out why she doesn't like the courses.
   ○ Only go to classes three days a week.

5. Write two or more sentences to explain why the answer you picked in Question 3 is the best first step for Joe.

   ____
   ____
   ____
   ____
   ____

6. Write two or more sentences to explain why the answer you picked in Question 4 is the best first step for Mary.

   ____
   ____
   ____
   ____
   ____

Words to Remember

future	**motivation**	**realistic**	**short-term**
long-term			

Chapter 5

You and Your Family

Andy Asks Today's Question: What has your family done for you?

Ben Martin, age 40, pilot
They have done everything for me. Stood behind me. Helped me with my education. Told me I could make it. I couldn't have gotten where I am without them.

Anna Noguchi, age 28, carpenter
Not much. I had to pay my own way from the time I was eighteen. I had six brothers and sisters. We all learned to help ourselves. Our folks taught us to be honest and to work hard. We've all turned out pretty well.

John Teller, age 19, student
They paid my way. They're still doing it. They're all back home working hard so I can get through school. They say it's worth every penny. It makes me feel important. But it's hard on me, too. I work as hard as I can in school. I want to do well and pay them back some day.

Charles Wiggins, age 22, waiter
They nag me. They're always after me. They always want me to do something different from what I'm doing. My older brother is a teacher. My parents want me to be a teacher, too. But I'm different from him. One of these days they'll figure that out.

Megan Green, age 24, job seeker
They just loved me. My family wasn't special. We didn't have a lot of money. We didn't take special trips together. But we all cared about each other. If anyone was in trouble, we all helped. It's still that way. We all count on each other.

There are a lot of different things that people get from their families. Feelings, habits, rules for living—these are things that families pass on. The answers to Andy's question that these people gave show that families play a big part in how successful people feel.

Words to Learn

relationships connections or ties between people

Learning Self-Image

There are many different kinds of families. Your family might have been a mother, father, brother, and sister. It might have been just one parent and you. It might have included a grandparent. It might have included a babysitter who was like a parent to you. The people who took care of you when you were very young were the first group you belonged to. You had your first important **relationships** with them. A relationship is the way in which people are connected to each other. Each person has many different relationships with other people.

In all your relationships, you find out what other people expect of you and what they think of you. That is why a lot of your self-image comes from the people around you. If they see you as doing well, they give you positive messages. These messages are rewards that make you feel good about yourself. When you get messages that you are not living up to what is expected of you, you feel bad.

You started to get messages from your family before you learned to talk. When you first learned to stand up or wave good-bye, the people around you were pleased. They gave you rewards for what you did. These early rewards might have been smiles, hugs, or extra attention. The rewards made you feel good and successful. They let you know that you were important to the people around you.

As you got older, you had more grown-up ways of building your self-image. In school, you got messages about how you were doing from teachers and from the other students. But your family was still important. They took an interest in you that your teachers and friends didn't take. You have a special place in your family. For many years the family provides a place where you can feel comfortable and safe.

Learning Attitudes

Just as you get your first ideas about yourself from your family, you also get ideas about the rest of the world from them. Many attitudes are learned from the family. Most people learn attitudes without knowing it. Children watch the adults around them. They learn to act the way the adults act. At the same time, the children are learning to think the way the adults think. The way adults solve problems, treat other people, or set the rules of the house are all learned by children.

Attitudes help people to set their goals. If good grades were important to your family, you might have set goals to get those grades. If getting a good job was more important in your family, you might have set goals that would lead to the job you wanted. Even when you set your own goals, those goals often show what you have learned from your family.

Why do you learn so much from your family? The connection you have with your family is not like your connection with anyone else. When you were first learning, you were with your family every day. You needed them for everything: food, clothes, shelter, love. They were not only the most important people in your life; they were the *only* people in your life. When you were older, you had relationships outside the family. But you still counted on the family to be there when you came home. In many ways the relationships in a family don't change. You are a son or daughter, a brother or sister, for life. No matter what you say or do, you still have those connections. For these reasons, the ties you have with your family are very strong. Most people cannot break those ties, even if they want to or need to when they are older.

Words to Learn

independent not guided or controlled by others

peers people your own age who often share your interests and with whom you spend a lot of time

Moving Away from the Family

At the same time you are enjoying a feeling of belonging to your family, you are learning to stand on your own and be **independent.** Being independent is also important for your self-confidence. Just as you can't have a big success every day, you can't get all the support you want from others every day. You have to learn to think about yourself as being successful. And you have to learn to make your own decisions and plan your own life.

From the time you were a baby, you have been learning about dependent and independent relationships. Babies are not at all independent. They must have everything done for them. As they grow, they learn to do things for themselves, little by little. Through their early teens, people get more and more independent from the family. They get closer and closer to their **peers.** They begin to depend on their peers for the rewards of belonging and feeling successful.

During this time, most people begin to change some of the ideas they have grown up with. They take on some of the attitudes and goals of their peers. They also make decisions about the things they have learned from their families. They might decide that some of their families' attitudes are negative. They might have new beliefs that are different from their families' beliefs. Here are some examples of the kinds of changes people make as they become independent of their families.

Words to Learn

balance to be even on both sides

Jack's family holds a strong belief that Jack thinks is wrong. They do not like people who are different from themselves. When Jack left home to work in another city, his first new friend was a man from another country. Jack knew that his parents would not want him to spend time with this man. But Jack knows that his friend is a fine person. He does not think the same way his family does.

Martha's mother has had a difficult life. She has always had to work hard. Her health has been poor. She feels and acts sad most of the time. Every time something goes wrong, she says it is because of her health. Martha has grown up with this attitude. She has learned to be negative about herself. Now a friend has started to talk to Martha about her problem. Martha sees that she must change her attitude. She must stop telling herself that she is unlucky and start to work for the things she wants. She must break away from her mother's way of thinking.

Jack and Martha have a difficult time ahead of them. They have to break away from ideas and attitudes that they have learned from their families. If you have to make a change like that, you need to be careful. You need to keep a **balance** between being part of a family and being independent. You don't have to break away from people just because you disagree with some of their ideas. For most people it is very important to keep getting positive messages from their families.

You may disagree with your family about many things. You may need to live on your own, away from them. But they are still the first people you loved and depended on. It still feels good to get along with them.

Finding the Right Balance

Throughout your life you will work on a balance in your relationship with your family. You need their support. But you also need your independence. You may have to change the way you act with your family from time to time to keep the relationship healthy. Here are some steps you can take to help keep the relationship with your family positive.

Think about what you have learned from your family. Take some time to make a list of the things your family has taught you. Your list might include beliefs, goals, attitudes, and even small habits that don't seem very important. Some of the things might be good and some bad.

Focus on the positive things. Think of the items on your list that seem positive to you. These are the things that have helped you. They might be long-term goals, such as finishing school. They might be habits, such as being on time or listening carefully to others. Be sure to keep these positive things in your life.

Try to change the negative things. Think about the negative items on your list. These things might be habits you formed when you were a child. The oldest habits can be the hardest to break, so you will have to work hard on these. Make a plan for working on each negative item. Use the steps in Chapters 1 through 4 when you can. For example, suppose one of your negative items was setting goals that are not realistic. The suggestions at the end of Chapter 4 can help you work on changing the way you set goals.

Try to understand your family's feelings. You might feel that your mother treats you like a baby, or that your father is too strict. You might have a brother or sister who always seems to do better than you. Remember that all these people are connected to you in a special way. They all care about you. They don't want to hurt you. They want to help. When they do something that bothers you, think about why they are doing it. Try to see them as people with their own ideas and their own problems. If you can understand them, it will help you understand how to deal with them.

Try to understand the part you are playing. How does your family see you? Are you hard on others? Do you expect others to do things that you should do for yourself? Think about your own part in family relationships. Be as honest as you can. You might be able to solve some problems by changing your attitude toward them.

Keep talking to your family. Let your family know what is going on in your life. Listen when they talk to you. When problems come up in the family, talk about them, too. Don't cut yourself off from family members.

Don't give up on family relationships. What do you do if you have a family problem that you can't seem to solve? Don't give up. Some terrible family relationships can become healthy again. For some people, it takes years. Some people have to be away from their families and rejoin them again when they are older. If you are having a problem with a family member, talk to older friends or to an aunt, uncle, or grandparent whom you can trust. Find out how they have solved the same kind of problem. Form close relationships with peers so that you will have the support you need while you are working on your family relationships. And keep an open mind. There is always hope for better relationships in the future.

Exercises

1. Look at the Words to Remember on this page. Then fill in each blank below with the right word that completes the sentence.

    a. As you grow up, you depend more and more on your ______________ for rewards and feelings of success.

    b. Throughout your life you have different ______________ with people you get to know well.

    c. Everyone needs both a feeling of belonging and of being ______________ .

2. Darken the circle next to each right answer. Good relationships with your family ______________ .

    ○ are good for your self-image
    ○ can help you get along with people outside your family
    ○ are important even when you are an adult
    ○ means that you agree with all your family's ideas

3. Darken the circle next to each true statement below.

    ○ All you need for confidence are good relationships with your family.
    ○ By the time you are twenty-one, you don't need your family anymore.
    ○ As you grow and change, your relationships with your family change, too.
    ○ As you grow up, your peers give you some of the support that your family once did.

4. Darken the circle next to the *best* answer. Carl has taken a job that his father doesn't think is right for him. His father tells him every day that Carl has made a big mistake. Carl's father probably ______ .

    ○ wants Carl to fail
    ○ wants the best for Carl
    ○ wants Carl never to leave home
    ○ wants Carl's job for himself

5. Darken the circle next to the *best* answer. Carl feels awful about his father's attitude. He wants to do something to solve the problem. Carl should try to ______ .

    ○ move away from his father as soon as possible
    ○ quit his job just to please his father
    ○ have an honest talk with his father about the problem
    ○ take his father to work with him

Words to Remember

balance **independent** **peers** **relationships**

Chapter 6
You're Not Alone

My brother Dave is a good person. Sometimes he has trouble getting down to work. He loves a good time. But when you have a problem, Dave is there to help. He really cares about people. I look up to him a lot.

Shelley Jackson

My nephew Dave is one of my favorite kids. He's full of ideas. Always thinking about his next step. He has tried lots of different jobs to learn all he can about the restaurant business. I think he'll do well.

Marge Tucker

Dave Jackson is a good worker. He gets along well with other people. I liked having him work here during the summers while he was in school.

Eve Sanders
Manager, Sanders' Diner

Dave Jackson was a nice kid who seemed to have a way with people. He was well-liked in school. In my class, he was very quiet. His work was mostly average or a little above average.

Ron Steen
English teacher, Westview High School

I've known Dave since we were both six years old. He's a good friend. Some people think that he's not very serious. But that's sort of an act. Dave has some good ideas. He works hard on the things he wants.

Ted Sutton

Jackson is quiet. That's because he's hardly ever in his apartment. He doesn't give anyone any trouble. Always pays his rent on time.

Joan Wright
Manager, Westview Apartments

All of these people are talking about the same man: Dave Jackson. These people all see Dave different ways. That is because they all have different relationships with him. These are just a few of the people who know Dave. There are many more who all have different connections with him.

Words to Learn

unwritten rules rules that are not written down but that most people go by and expect others to follow

Different Kinds of Relationships

Think about all the different relationships you have. Some are stronger than others. Some last a lifetime, while others last a few months or years. Some are based on friendships while others are just business. No matter what the relationships are, you want them to be successful.

Having successful relationships is one of the most important ways you have of feeling self-confident. Building good relationships is a skill that you learn, starting when you are very young.

As you read in Chapter 5, your family were the first ones who showed you how to get along with other people. They taught you to be polite, to share with others, and so on. As you grew up, you had more people to teach you the rules that everyone lives by. In school, you have to follow the directions your teachers give. But there are many other rules that you learn to follow. These may be called **unwritten rules.** They are not listed anywhere. You learn them just by going through life.

In a classroom, some unwritten rules might be: Treat other students fairly. Don't tell the teacher every time someone bothers you. Don't brag. When you follow these rules, you get rewards. You fit in with the group and you are liked. If you don't follow the rules, you may be left out.

When you get to be a teenager, your peers become very important. You are getting more independent of your family. You find that people your age seem to understand your ideas and your feelings.

They are a group you can feel close to as you are moving away from your family. But after a while, you'll find you need some independence from your peers, too. You can still have good friends. You may ask for their advice often. But you must also make up your own mind about how to live your life.

More Independence

If you depend too much on your family, you have trouble growing up. You can't take your place in the adult world. If you depend too much on your peers, you don't learn to stick up for your own ideas. You might do or say things that you don't believe in. If that happens, your self-image will suffer. It is often hard to find the right balance between being part of a group and being independent. Everyone has to find the balance that works best in his or her life.

After high school, the rules that you live by keep changing. You might move to a different city to go to college or take a job. Even if you stay in the same place, you will be making changes in your relationships. For example, at work everyone has to think first about getting the job done. Rules that were important in high school may not be important any longer. Instead, there are new rules about how to act with the people where you work. If you're going to do well, you have to learn to follow these rules at the same time you are learning to do your job. A time like this can be hard on a person's self-confidence. The "at home" and safe feelings that the family once provided may seem far away.

The independence that you have been learning through the years is important when you go through a big change. You have to count on yourself to learn new rules, to use new skills, and to get along with new people. Every success you have in forming good relationships with different people will give you more confidence. Following the steps on page 41 can help make all your relationships more successful.

Understand the different kinds of relationships you have. For all the different kinds of relationships you have, there are different sets of rules. Try to understand these differences. For example, you look up to a teacher or a boss. They are interested in the kind of work you can do. But you probably wouldn't share private feelings with them as you would with a close friend. Keep in mind the unwritten rules that go with all of your relationships.

Be friendly. Keep in mind the kinds of things that friends do for each other. Make sure you do these things for the people around you. Give help when you can. Give others the positive messages that everyone needs in order to feel confident. When you give these things, you will get them in return.

Give other people credit. Give the people around you credit for their ideas and beliefs. Never give the idea that you don't think much of them just because they don't agree with your ideas. Listen carefully to what people say. Try to understand their thoughts and their feelings. It's okay to disagree. But you can do it in a friendly way.

Don't take everything personally. Do you sometimes feel that others don't like you? Do you often feel left out? You might be taking things too personally—thinking that people are doing things to you or because of you. Chances are that no one is trying to hurt you. If you put aside hurt feelings and act friendly, you will get along with others better.

When something goes wrong, talk about it. If you have a problem with someone important to you, it is a good idea to talk to him or her about it. First make sure you understand the problem. Then find a time when you can talk in private. Explain the problem as you see it. Listen carefully to what the other person says. Don't expect to solve a problem with one talk. Your goals should be to talk honestly and to understand each other.

When you're angry, wait. When you are really angry at someone try to calm down before you talk about it. Think about why you are angry. Think about the best thing to do. When you are calm, talk to the person. It is often surprising how easy it is to talk out a problem that seemed terrible when it first came up.

Don't expect to win all the time. When you disagree with someone, sometimes you will be right. Sometimes the other person will be right. Sometimes you will have to leave things as they are, as a friendly disagreement. You don't always have to be right. Learn to back off when necessary to keep things friendly.

Forgive other people. Don't stay angry. If you have talked about a problem and you still feel very angry, try to make yourself stop. Anger that goes on for a long time is hard on you. Anger is a negative feeling. It can keep you from working on the positive parts of your life.

Use your sense of humor. One of the best tools for getting along with people is a sense of humor. This doesn't mean that you can turn any problem into a joke. But a joke can often help to make people calm down and look at a problem in a different way. Try not to be serious all the time. Learn to see the lighter side of life.

Exercises

1. Darken the circle next to each right answer. Which of the following are examples of unwritten rules?
   - ○ Don't interrupt when your boss is talking.
   - ○ Be on time for work each day.
   - ○ Don't act glad when someone else has a problem.
   - ○ Always wear safety glasses when they are needed.
   - ○ Don't say bad things about other people when they are not around.

2. Darken the circle next to the *best* answer. Why does everyone see you a little differently?
   - ○ Everyone sees you in the way you touch his or her life.
   - ○ People change their minds from day to day.
   - ○ Some days are sunny and some days are cloudy.
   - ○ All people have different eyesight.

3. Darken the circle next to the *best* answer. In all your relationships you have to find a balance between ______ .
   - ○ laughing and crying
   - ○ belonging and being independent
   - ○ following rules and breaking rules
   - ○ morning and night

4. Darken the circle next to the *best* answer. Ann has always felt that she cannot make friends. A few years ago Ann made one good friend. She felt that she didn't have to make any more friends. Now her good friend is moving away. What should Ann do?
   - ○ Ann should get used to being alone. She should be completely independent.
   - ○ Since she can't make friends, Ann should put all her energy into her job.
   - ○ Ann should learn to be friendly to the people around her, so they will know she can be a friend.
   - ○ Ann should move to where her friend is moving.

5. Write two or more sentences to explain what advice you would give Ann in Question 4 to help her become more friendly with other people.

   ____

   ____

   ____

   ____

   ____

   ____

   ____

Words to Remember

unwritten rules

Chapter 7

The Changes You Go Through

Joan could hardly believe the good news. Her husband Curt had just told her that he had decided not to take the new job in Chicago, Illinois. He had found a better job right here in Cartersville, Virginia. For weeks Joan had been fearing the move to Chicago. She knew that the job there was an important step for Curt. He had said that he really had no choice but to move.

Joan had grown up in Cartersville. Her whole family was there. Joan counted on them for support and company. Her mother even helped take care of Joan's daughter while Joan worked part-time. Joan hated the idea of being far away from her family. She felt as if she would be alone and isolated in Chicago. Curt would have his new job to keep him busy. But what would there be for Joan to do in a strange new place?

Now everything was okay again. Joan and Curt talked happily about his change of plans. Joan didn't hear the details. She thought about calling her parents and sisters to tell them she was staying.

Suddenly a loud ringing sound cut through her thoughts. Was it the phone? Joan felt confused. Then she realized what the sound was. She reached over and turned off the alarm. Slowly she climbed out of bed.

The good news had been only a dream. Joan looked at the stacks of boxes, books, and clothing in her room. Today she would finish packing. Thinking about her dream, Joan blinked back tears. She had never felt so sad in her life.

Joan was facing a big change. It was not her choice. It happened to her. She was scared because so many parts of her life would be affected by the change. The biggest part would be her relationships with other people. She would be far away from her family and friends. She would have no connections in the new city.

Joan also wondered if she would be able to find a part-time job in Chicago. In her hometown, she worked for an old family friend. No one in Chicago would know her the way her old boss did. She would have to look for a new job. She would have to find day care for her daughter. She would have to find out where to shop for food, clothing and things for the house. All of these things together seemed like more than she could handle.

Why Change Is Hard

Most people have to face some big changes during their lives. Such things as moving, changing jobs, or getting married are all common changes that most people go through. Any big change affects a part of your life that is important to your self-confidence. Important relationships with other people may be changed or broken off. You may have to build new skills or use your skills in a different way.

Words to Learn

control the power to make something go the way you want it to

You may have to change goals that you had set. When you change any of the things that you need for self-confidence, you often feel shaky and unsure of yourself.

Why does change have to be hard on confidence? When your life is going smoothly, you have a feeling of **control.** You know what to expect. Nothing gets away from you or surprises you. You might be bored some of the time, but you don't have to worry about strange new problems. Control over certain things can be very helpful. It's good to have control over your feelings and attitudes, for example. That gives you some control over many parts of your life.

You might wish that you could keep control over all the important parts of your life and not let changes happen to you. But that is not possible. Everyone has to go through some big changes in a lifetime. Some of the changes come suddenly, such as a move to a new city. Some changes take years to happen, such as the changes a person goes through as he or she becomes more and more independent. Some of the changes happen to you, and some you choose.

Often change is good. For example, your relationship with your parents changes as you become independent. This is good for you. This change prepares you to take care of yourself. You might change jobs in order to get more pay or better training. You might change from being single to being part of a couple. You might decide to become a parent. These are changes that people go through because they choose to. But they can still be difficult.

When you make a change, you can't be sure how it will work out. You can think about the future and make plans for it, but no one can know exactly what will happen. You may be sure that your new job will pay more. But you can't be sure that you will like what you'll be doing. You may be sure of where you will live in a new town. But you can't be sure that you will be happy there. You may be sure that you want to be a parent. But you can't be sure of what raising children will be like. Everyone wonders if he or she will be good enough to do each new job in life well.

Attitude and Action

How can you get through the changes you have to go through? You can use the ideas about attitude that you read about in Chapter 2. If every change makes you nervous and afraid, maybe you have a negative attitude toward change. If you feel sure that each change will go badly, you don't have the confidence to make it go well. You will be working against yourself.

The key to making changes work well for you is to take positive action. Often if you can see that a change is coming, you can start to get ready for it. For example, suppose you think that the company you work for may go out of business. You can start to find out about other places where you might work. You can think about different kinds of jobs you can do. You might end up making a change yourself, before a change is forced on you. If you have to make a change, it's always better if you can make plans to get ready for it.

Joan felt that she was stuck with her change. She couldn't change the facts about Curt's new job. In many ways, it was important to her that he take the job. She and Curt decided that together. But after that, Joan felt that she was stuck with the change. She felt that control was taken away from her and that she was not important any more. But Joan could do something to help herself. She could work on her attitude toward the move. She could think of ways to make the move easier.

For example, she could start to learn all about Chicago. She might find out the names of a few people she could contact there. She could call or write to those people for more information before she moved. She could make a resume for herself—a list of the jobs she has held and the skills she can offer in a new job. She could get a letter of recommendation from her boss to take with her. She could even plan to have one of her family visit her after she moved. These actions would give her something to look forward to as she goes through a difficult time. They would give her some feeling of confidence about the coming change.

Taking Control

When a big change comes to your life, you often feel out of control. And in some ways, you *may* be out of control. If your parents move while you are living with them, you can't control that. If the boss who has helped you succeed at work suddenly leaves, you can't control that. But you can control the way you feel and act when you are faced with change. Here are some steps that can help you get through a change successfully.

Figure out how big the change is. "*Nothing* will be the same again." "I'll *never* get used to things this way." If you have thoughts like these, stop yourself. Think about the change you are going through. Often a change looks bigger than it really is. A new boss, a new home, or a change in a relationship may be easier to get used to than you think it will be. Be as honest with yourself as you can about how big and important each change is.

Figure out what you can and cannot control. Try to divide up the change into the parts that you can do something about and the parts that you can't do anything about. Think carefully about the ways in which you can take action to make things better. Make a list of things you can do. Some of these things may be very simple. You might begin to work on a new resume, make a phone call to get some information, or just talk to a friend about your feelings.

Words to Learn

accept to get used to something or to agree to something

Try to accept the things you can't control. Most people spend a lot of time and energy trying to change things that cannot be changed. This is as useless as setting goals that cannot be reached. When you work at something you cannot do, you are bound to fail. Often people try it anyway, because it's so hard to **accept** a change that they dislike or fear. Work as hard as you can on the things you can control. That will help you to accept the things you can't.

Think about the things you can hold on to. There are some things that you can keep from changing: a positive attitude, your goals and beliefs, the good relationships you have with other people. Keep these things in mind when you are going through changes. Stay in touch with people who are important to you. Keep working toward your goals, even if they must be changed. *Have confidence in yourself.*

Remember that these steps won't keep you from having to go through changes. Everyone has to face them. But taking these steps can help give you more control over your life. They can help you feel good about yourself even if you don't like some of the changes that you will have to make in your life.

Exercises

1. Look at the Words to Remember on this page. Then fill in each blank below with the right word that completes the sentence.

   a. If you can't do anything about a problem, you have to ______________ it.

   b. If you are making a change, you can still keep a feeling of ______________ over your life.

2. Darken the circle next to each right answer. Which of the following things can you control?

   ○ your attitude
   ○ your boss's ideas
   ○ where your friends live
   ○ your goals

3. Darken the circle next to each statement that is true.

   ○ You can stop change from happening if you try hard enough.
   ○ Everyone goes through some big changes in a lifetime.
   ○ Some changes can be difficult but can be good for you at the same time.
   ○ When *you* decide to make a change, it is always easy.

4. Darken the circle next to the *best* answer.

   Ed's boss offered him a new job that will pay more money. Ed knows it will be harder than the job he has now. He is not sure he can handle the new job. What should Ed do?

   ○ Look for a job where he will never have to change.
   ○ Tell his boss he'd like to wait a year and then take the new job.
   ○ Build his confidence so that he won't be so afraid of the new job.
   ○ Take a vacation so that he will be well rested before taking the new job.

5. Christine is living with her sister and brother-in-law. Christine will have to move soon because her sister is going to have a baby. She has to find a new apartment and a roommate to help pay the rent. Christine is happy for her sister but upset by this change in *her* life. Write two or more sentences to explain what steps Christine could take to help make this change a good one.

   ____
   ____
   ____
   ____
   ____
   ____

Words to Remember

accept **control**

Chapter 8

Your Biggest Problems

Mark feels tired all the time. He has been spending all his time and energy trying to solve a big problem. Because of an illness, Mark has lost his hearing. He has been learning to read lips and to use sign language. It has been hard to do these things and keep up with the rest of his life at the same time. In spite of all his work, life is very hard for Mark.

Sometimes Mark doesn't know if it's worth it. He thinks he might just stop trying to solve his problem and stay at home—for the rest of his life.

Mark knows that he can't change back to the way he was before he lost his hearing. But he finds it very hard to accept the change. He feels as if it has made a mess of his whole life. Right now he can't do his job. His plans for the future have all changed. He can't move forward until he learns to use sign language and lipreading. His relationships have changed, too. His family and friends want to help, but they don't know what to do. People who don't know Mark well stay away from him. They act as if they're afraid of him. Mark feels like some sort of monster. His self-image is as low as it has ever been.

Words to Learn

crisis a time of serious trouble or danger

isolated to be cut off, or all alone

support group people who help others to deal with a certain kind of problem

Feelings in a Crisis

Mark is going through a **crisis.** Everyone has to face crises at some time. Some examples of a crisis are a very bad illness, the death of a loved one, a terrible accident, or being hooked on drugs or alcohol. If any of these things happen to you or to someone close to you, it can change your life. The change might last for a while, or it might last forever.

Like any other change, a crisis gives you a new set of problems you have never faced before. But problems like Mark's are bigger than most. Dealing with a crisis can take up all of a person's time and energy. People who are going through a crisis often find it very difficult to take care of a job or make plans or keep up with the other people in their lives. They might feel as if they are slipping backward, no matter how hard they try to solve their problems.

Most people feel lonely and **isolated** at a time like this. They don't know how to handle all the problems that go with a crisis. Their friends are not going through the same problems. It is easy to feel as if no one else in the world is facing the same hard work and the same feelings of unhappiness and fear.

Support in a Crisis

If you are facing a crisis, you need to accept one basic fact: you need help to get through it. One of the main kinds of help is a **support group.** Have you ever had a problem that troubled you or embarrassed you so much that you couldn't tell anyone you knew about it? Support groups can give you a place to talk about your problem. They let you know that a number of other people have the same problem.

Words to Learn

experts people who know a lot about a certain thing

models people who serve as examples you can copy and learn from

You can be sure that people who share your problem understand your feelings and your needs. Sometimes, just knowing you are not alone is the first step toward getting through a crisis.

Support groups also are important because the people who run them are **experts** at working on one kind of problem. They are trained to help. Often support groups introduce you to people who have made it through the same problem you have. These people are **models.** They are living proof that it is possible to get through a difficult time and then build a new life. They can give advice that really works. And they can help others believe that it is possible to regain control of their lives. Here is an example of the help a support group gave one young woman going through a family crisis.

Anna's mother became addicted to pain pills after an operation. At first Anna was ashamed. She didn't want anyone to know. She stopped asking her friends over to her house. She stayed home from school a lot. Finally the school counselor told Anna about a support group for students whose parents had the same problem Anna's mother had. At first Anna didn't want to go. She thought her mother would be angry. She thought that she wouldn't fit in with the group. But when she finally went, she found that the group understood her and cared about her.

After a while Anna was able to talk to her mother about getting help. Anna's mother *was* angry. It was a long time before she took Anna's advice. But Anna had help for herself during this difficult time. And she was not ashamed or alone anymore. She began to get her own life under control.

Then Anna went through a different period. She had to pay attention to the things in her life that she had ignored, such as her school work and her friends. After a year in the group Anna thought that she didn't need to go anymore. But she still wanted to be with them. When she felt sad or angry about the things she had missed, the group members understood. So Anna kept going to the group. After a while she saw that new members looked to her for help. As she became a model for these people, Anna found a new confidence that was very good for her.

Anna found that she had to live with her problem even after the crisis seemed to be over. The feelings that went with the crisis changed, but they did not go away. Anna learned to live with the feelings. She learned how to become a strong, confident person again.

Some of the steps you can take to deal with the biggest problems in your life are the same as those in Chapter 7. But there are other steps you can take when you face problems that change your life in a bigger way.

Name the problem. This can be a scary step. People don't like to admit, even to themselves, that they have problems they cannot solve. Be as realistic and honest as you can. You can't start to solve a problem until you face it. If someone close to you has a problem that is making your life difficult, try to understand all parts of the problem. For example, Anna's mother had the problem of being addicted to drugs. As her daughter, Anna had her own problems: shame, mixed feelings for her mother, and a low self-image were just a few of them.

Find some help. Start by getting ideas from people you trust. If you are in school, a **counselor** might be able to help you. You also can talk to a minister or rabbi. Your doctor or a good friend or someone in your family might have ideas about ways to get help. If you don't know anyone or don't want to talk to someone you know, look in your telephone book. Look under the name of the county or town you live in for headings such as Family Health Services, Human Resources, or Social Services. Look in the general section under headings such as Crisis, Suicide, Alcohol, Family, Child Abuse, or Health. A Family Services Association can help with many kinds of problems. If you have a problem with the law, call the Legal Aid Society.

Words to Learn

counselor someone who has knowledge and training on how to help people solve their problems

Under some of these headings you will find more than one listing. If you are not sure which listing is right for you, call the County Department of Health. Explain your problem. They will give you a number to call. Write down all the information and numbers you are given. Whatever you do, don't give up. You *will* be able to find help.

Use the help you find. You probably will be nervous about going to the first meeting with a counselor or support group. Everyone feels this way. Make yourself go. When you get advice, do your best to follow it. Don't wait and see if the problem will go away. Serious problems only get worse if you don't act to help yourself.

Be positive about the future. When you feel your lowest, you have to believe that things can be okay again. There is no better way to do this than to watch and listen to people who have been through your problem. They know how to share their confidence when you don't feel confident on your own.

When you are at a low point, think about changes for the better that you have made. Keep trying to move in the right direction. You may take small steps at first, but those small steps add up. Every step you take will give you a little more courage to go on. Sometimes the greatest courage is in just getting through the day, no matter how tired and sad you are. Give yourself credit every day for your ability to keep going.

Exercises

1. Look at the Words to Remember on this page. Then fill in each blank below with the right word that completes the sentence.

   a. A ______________ is a serious problem that changes your life in a big way.

   b. A ______________ gives advice about solving problems.

   c. A ______________ is made up of people who can help you feel less isolated with your problem.

2. Darken the circle next to the *best* answer. A really serious problem ______ .

   ○ will never be solved
   ○ might be with you for many years
   ○ should not be talked about
   ○ will not happen to you if you are careful

3. Darken the circle next to each right answer. A good support group ______ .

   ○ can show you that people live through your problem
   ○ can give you the company of people who understand you
   ○ can solve your problem for you
   ○ can help in different ways at different times

4. Gene said, "I'm working as hard as I can on my problem. But for every two steps I take forward, I take one step back. I feel as if I'm failing." Write two or more sentences to explain what you think Gene means by this. What advice would you give him if he were your friend?

   ____

   ____

   ____

   ____

   ____

   ____

5. Look in your telephone book to find help with the problems listed below. Then write the name and phone number on the line next to the problem. Try to find at least one listing for each.

   alcoholism ______________________

   mental illness ______________________

   child abuse ______________________

   trouble with the law ______________________

   drug addiction ______________________

Words to Remember

counselor
crisis
experts
isolated
models
support group

Posttest

1. Darken the circle next to the *best* answer. Which of the following is the best definition of self-confidence?

   ○ Self-confidence is being liked by everyone around you.

   ○ Self-confidence is having a positive attitude about yourself and your abilities.

   ○ Self-confidence is feeling that you are better than all of the people around you.

   ○ Self-confidence is always knowing how to handle a new problem.

2. Below are five phrases that have to do with self-confidence. Below them are five statements made by different people. On the blank next to each phrase write the letter of the statement that best matches it.

   ______ knowing your skills
   ______ belonging and being independent
   ______ negative attitude
   ______ dealing with change
   ______ realistic goals

   a. "No matter how hard I try, I can't seem to learn the new filing system at work. I've been at it for two days. I've decided to quit before my boss fires me."

   b. "As soon as I graduate from high school next June I'm going to join the Air Force. They have a good training program for flight mechanics. Someday I hope to work for a big airline company repairing their giant jets."

   c. "I'm sure I can do this job, sir. I feel I'm well-organized, good with numbers, and know how to deal with the public."

   d. "I thought my parents would give me a hard time because I want to get my own apartment. But they were pretty understanding. I guess they know I'm still going to see them a lot. After all, they're my family."

   e. "I sure wasn't prepared for this. First the college said I would get a part scholarship. Now they say it was a mistake. I have to pay all the tuition myself. I'll have to get a part-time job to get the money. This really is causing me a lot of problems."

3. Suppose you have all the problems listed below. Which one should you begin to work on *first*? Darken the circle next to it. Then write one or more sentences explaining the reasons for your answer.

   ○ You and a family member haven't gotten along in months.

   ○ You feel you need to improve your job skills.

   ○ Your attitude is negative most of the time.

   ○ You're not making progress toward a long-term goal.

   ____
   ____
   ____
   ____
   ____
   ____

Use the information you learned in Chapters 2, 4, and 7 to help you complete the following.

4. In Chapter 2 you read about how a positive attitude is important in building self-confidence. Think of a problem you faced in the last six months. Tell whether you looked at it with a negative or positive attitude. If it was positive, describe the steps you took to solve the problem. If it was negative, tell how you might go about changing your attitude the next time you're faced with the same kind of problem.

5. Chapter 4 discussed how important setting and reaching good goals is in building confidence. Think of three *short-term* goals you set in the past that you may or may not have reached. If you reached your goals, explain how doing so might help you one day in reaching one of your *long-term* goals. If you did not, explain what steps you might take next time to try and reach your goals.

6. In Chapter 7 you learned why the changes we all go through can sometimes be very hard. Think of one big change you went through in the past year or two. Tell whether or not you remained *in control* while you went through the change. If you did, explain how you felt you were able to do that. If you didn't, explain what steps you could take the next time to stay in control when you're faced with a big change.

Answers to Exercises

Chapter 1

1. a. confidence (or self-confidence)
   b. ability
   c. self-image
2. hard work
3. Answers may vary, but the following should be noted:
   a. Everyone needs the feeling of belonging that good friends can give. When others like you, it helps you to like yourself.
   b. When you do a job well, you use your skills. This helps you to see your abilities and to feel successful.
   c. Your plans give you something to work for. They give you a chance to prove to yourself that you can be successful.
4. Answers may vary, but the following should be noted. When you have success, you feel good about yourself. Others look up to you. This helps you go on to be successful again.

Chapter 2

1. a. attitude
   b. positive
   c. solution
2. your self-image
3. want to change; take action
4. I know now why I made that mistake at work today.
   I never did like school, but I know I need a high school diploma in order to get a good job.
5. Answers may vary, but it should be noted that you can make life bad for yourself if you have a negative attitude. Your own attitude can work against you just as a real enemy might.

Chapter 3

1. a. skills
   b. compliments
2. a positive self-image; to know that you have skills
3. plan a job ahead of time; understand written directions; know which tools to use; solve problems that you don't expect
4. Answers will vary. It should be noted that it is important to keep trying new things or new ways of using old skills. In order to believe in yourself, you have to stay active and keep trying.
5. Answers will vary.

Chapter 4

1. a. realistic
   b. motivation
   c. Long-term
2. you believe in; are realistic
3. List the steps leading to the goal.
4. figure out why she doesn't like the courses
5. Answers may vary, but it should be noted that if Joe lists the steps leading to the goal first, he will have a better idea of whether the goal is realistic and right for him. He shouldn't make any other plans until he is sure about this goal.
6. Answers may vary, but it should be noted that Mary has to decide *why* she doesn't like her courses before she decides whether or not to continue in nursing. If she decides that she really does not want to be a nurse, she shouldn't force herself to take courses she won't use.

Chapter 5

1. a. peers
   b. relationships
   c. independent
2. are good for your self-image; can help you get along with people outside your family; are important even when you are an adult
3. As you grow and change, your relationships with your family change, too.
   As you grow up, your peers give you some of the things that your family once did.
4. wants the best for Carl
5. have an honest talk with his father about the problem

Chapter 6

1. Don't interrupt when your boss is talking.
   Don't act glad when someone else has a problem.
   Don't say bad things about other people when they are not around.
2. Everyone sees you in the way you touch his or her life.
3. belonging and being independent
4. Ann should learn to be friendly to the people around her so they will know she can be a friend.
5. Answers will vary.

Chapter 7

1. a. accept
   b. control
2. your attitude; your goals
3. Everyone goes through some big changes in a lifetime. Some changes can be difficult and good for you at the same time.
4. Build his confidence so that he won't be so afraid of the new job.
5. Answers will vary. It should be noted that Christine should think positive about the move. She could plan to decorate her new apartment in a way that she would like. Finding the right roommate can be difficult, but it would give her the opportunity to make a close friend. She should think about all the good points of having her own apartment and about planning a small party once she moves in. That would give her something to look forward to and make her feel in control.

Chapter 8

1. a. crisis
   b. counselor
   c. support group
2. might be with you for many years
3. can show you that people live through your problem; can give you the company of people who understand you; can help in different ways at different times
4. Answers will vary. It should be noted that Gene feels that his problem is getting worse even though he is working on it. Good advice for Gene is to work with a support group or a counselor. He might need to work on his problem in a different way.
5. Answers will vary.

Posttest

1. Self-confidence is having a positive attitude about yourself and your abilities.
2. knowing your skills: c
   belonging and being independent: d
   negative attitude: a
   dealing with change: e
   realistic goals: b
3. Your attitude is negative most of the time.
   If your attitude is negative, you will not be able to do a good job of solving your other problems. When you improve your attitude, you will be better at dealing with the other problems.
4. Answers will vary.
5. Answers will vary.
6. Answers will vary.